FOOD COMBINING SIMPLIFIED
How To Get The Most From Your Food

Dennis Nelson

Recipes by Pamela Cohn

Cover Design by Peggy McCarty

First Edition--1983
Second Revised Edition--1987
Third Revised Edition--1988

DEDICATION

To the spirit of Dr. Herbert M. Shelton (1895-1985), whose writings led me out of the confusion surrounding health matters, and into a new reality of body awareness, this booklet is gratefully dedicated.

ACKNOWLEDGEMENTS

The material contained in these pages is a simplified version of the original work presented by Dr. Herbert Shelton in his book, <u>Food</u> <u>Combining</u> <u>Made</u> <u>Easy</u>, first published in 1951. I wish to express my deep appreciation for this most significant work.

CONTENTS

Glossary..4

Introduction..5

The Rationale For "Food Combining"......................8

Digestion Explained...13

Classification of Foods...18

Incompatible Combinations..................................20

Fruit Eating..25

Meal Planning..30

Seasonal Menus...37

Closing Thoughts...39

Recipes..39-62

GLOSSARY

digestion--the conversion of food into simple substances in preparation for its assimilation into the bloodstream.

enzyme--a substance that acts as a catalyst in the digestion of food.

fermentation--the decomposition of carbohydrates (sugars and starches) and their conversion by microorganisms to poisonous substances.

gastric--pertaining to the stomach.

"natural hygiene"--a philosophy and lifestyle, ascertained by the study of all those factors and influences which affect our health.

nutrition--the sum total of all body processes which interact to supply our nutritive needs.

putrefaction-the decomposition of proteins and their conversion by microorganisms to poisonous substances.

INTRODUCTION

The term "food combining" refers to those combinations of foods which are compatible with each other in digestive chemistry. In other words, the goal of "food combining" is to aid the digestive process. This booklet will inform you of both compatible and incompatible food combinations. It will also guide you in selecting compatible food menus.

By applying these principles, your nutrition will be enhanced, as only food which is digested is capable of nourishing us. And, we avoid the poisonous biproducts of indigestion, along with its unpleasant symptoms.

Efficient digestion also has a beneficial influence on the body's energy level. The amount of energy expended to digest three conventional meals has been estimated to be the equivalent of eight hours of "working" energy. By selecting compatible food combinations, the digestive task is lessened, allowing more energy for other activities.

The fact that two billion dollars are spent annually on antacids in this country, testifies to the need for such information. The discomforts of indigestion are so common among our people that it's almost considered normal. And the incidence of various diseases of the digestive tract are increasing at an alarming rate. Rather than use drugs to suppress the symptoms of indigestion, it would be wiser to remove the causes of the indigestion. And then, apply those practices which favor good digestion. Simple meals of compatible combinations are a significant factor in maintaining good digestion.

The effects of feeding children the haphazard combinations of foods commonly offered, should also be considered. The fermentation produced in their digestive tract as a result of such eating represents a major factor in causing their diseases. Dr. Shelton comments on this in his book, <u>Food Combining Made Easy</u>: "Until parents learn how to feed their children with proper respect for enzymic limitations and cease feeding them the so-called 'balanced meals' now in vogue, their children are going to continue to suffer, not only with colds and tonsillar troubles, but with gastritis (indigestion), diarrhea, constipation, feverishness, the various children's diseases, poliomyelitis, etc."

Having suffered much of my own life from indigestion, I was elated to find Dr. Shelton's book in 1973. Since that time, I have proven for myself the truth of these dietary principles. And there are thousands of others who have done the same. Now it's up to you. Study these principles, and then put them into practice. If your own experience verifies the truth of this little book, then I encourage you to hold dearly to your new discovery.

THE RATIONALE FOR "FOOD COMBINING"

Throughout the century, physiologists have been conducting experiments relating to the digestion of food. They observed that the efficiency of digestion is greatly dependent upon the types of food combined at a meal. However, this information needed to be transferred from the laboratory to the kitchen if people were to benefit from it. This was accomplished by the doctors of the "natural hygiene" philosophy. They concluded that the human digestive system works best when meals are simple and combinations are minimal. This resulted in the principles of "food combining".

Dr. Shelton commented on this in his book: "As all physiologists are agreed that the character of the digestive juice secreted corresponds with the character of the food to be digested, and that each food calls for its own specific modification of the digestive juice, it follows as the night the day, that complex mixtures of food greatly impair the efficiency of digestion. Simple meals will prove to be more easily digested, hence more healthful."

These principles may be observed throughout the animal world. Carnivorous animals eat their meat alone, without any carbohydrate or acid foods. Birds and squirrels also choose one type of food at a meal. Certainly, no animal in nature makes their meal on such a variety of foods, as people are accustomed to eating at a conventional meal.

Now, to give you greater insight into why "food combining" works, let me present a familiar situation to you: You're reading a book. Suddenly the phone rings. If you try to continue reading the book while having the phone conversation, then both tasks become more difficult. Eventually, you'll probably decide to focus your attention on one or the other. Well, this situation is similar to how the human body digests food. If incompatible food combinations are taken at a meal, the attention your body is capable of giving to each type of food is reduced, and the digestion of each food is curtailed. "Food combining" stresses the importance of both simplicity and compatibility in meal planning.

Actually, the wonderful thing about "food combining" is that everyone may benefit from it. The digestive system works fundamentally the same for all of us. This is not to deny the fact that individuals vary in their capacity to digest food, but rather to dispute the argument that "food combining" principles are only helpful for particular people.

In the words of Dr. Shelton again: "There are great numbers of people who will object to these simple rules on the ground that their own experiences have revealed that it is safe for them to violate each and every one of these rules. The rules, they will say, may be applicable to some people, but not to them. The individual, rejecting the existence of a general law as the basis of physiology and digestion, in diet, in health and disease, and holding that what is most valuable to one person may not be helpful to another--that 'one man's meat is another man's poison'--and that what is best for each individual may be determined only by observation of the idiosyncrasies of each, will, perhaps, find it impossible to accept the truth of any plan of living that does not meet with the approval of his/her habits and prejudices.

"If we accept the obvious fact that a general law underlies physiology and biology and that all mankind are subject to this law, it becomes easy to understand that hard and fast rules may be established that will fit all human beings. Physiology is not as chaotic and unlawful as some people seem to think.

"I frequently get another objection to any effort to regulate the diet and eating practices according to any law of life. It runs this way: 'Diet is not all of life. Other things are also important.' Nobody stresses this fact as much or as soundly as does the Hygienist; but the objection is not raised by those who wish to emphasize the importance of the other factors of life. It is made by those who desire to find a reason to disregard all the sane rules of eating and of living."

Although "food combining" will aid the digestive process considerably, it will not guarantee good digestion. There are other factors which may reduce our digestive capacity. Such acts as overeating, eating under stressful conditions, eating when fatigued, eating just before or soon after strenuous exercise, and eating during strong emotional experiences, all hinder the digestive process. Also, whenever fever or inflammation are present, the digestive powers are diminished to conserve energy, and digestion is somewhat suspended. And, substances such as condiments (including salt), vinegar, alcohol, coffee, or tea all irritate the digestive tract and retard digestion considerably. All these factors must be considered if one desires good digestion, and consequently a well nourished body.

To complete this chapter, let's discuss a common objection to "food combining", stated as follows: All foods are composed of various nutritive materials and yet the human body is capable of digesting them. It seems that "nature" does not observe "food combining" principles.

The answer to this objection is this: The human digestive system is capable of adjusting itself to the digestion of individual natural foods, with appropriate timing of various enzymes and digestive juices. However, when two or more foods are combined haphazardly, the digestive limitations are exceeded and digestion is inevitably impaired. Apparently, the creations of the kitchen were not considered when the human digestive system was devised.

DIGESTION EXPLAINED

Digestion is the process by which the complex materials of food are broken down into simpler substances in preparation for their entrance into the bloodstream. For example, proteins are broken down into various amino acids; carbohydrates, composed of starches and sugars, are converted to glucose, a simple sugar; and fats are broken down into fatty acids. The body is then able to use these simpler materials to build new tissue. Let's look at this process in more detail.

The human digestive tract may be conveniently divided into three cavities--the mouth, the stomach, and the small intestine. Regarding the practical application of "food combining" principles, the conditions present in the mouth and stomach will be our primary concern. However, it should be understood that the efficiency of digestion, as it continues in the small intestine, is greatly dependent upon the work done in the mouth and stomach.

When food enters the mouth, it's masticated and mixed with saliva, initiating the digestive process. Appropriate digestive juices are also secreted here, according to the type of food ingested. If the food contains starch, then an enzyme, *salivary amylase*, is also secreted at this time. This enzyme is active only in the presence of starch and will not be secreted otherwise.

After leaving the mouth, the food passes down the esophagus and into the stomach. Here, gastric juice is secreted, containing primarily hydrochloric acid and digestive enzymes. The concentration of this hydrochloric acid varies, depending on the type of food ingested. Protein requires a highly acidic medium for the digestive enzyme, *pepsin*, to be effective. Starches and fats, however, require a nearly neutral medium for their digestion. In fact, *salivary amylase* is actually destroyed in the presence of a highly acidic gastric juice. And the enzyme, *gastric lipase*, secreted for fat digestion, is also inhibited in its work in the presence of a highly acidic medium. These distinctions represent a significant factor in complicating digestion.

A second factor to consider is this: Each cavity contains its own distinctive digestive secretions with which to carry on its own specific work of digestion. And at each stage of this process, digestion proceeds more or less efficiently depending upon the conditions present at each stage. In other words, the efficiency of digestion in the intestines is dependent upon the work done in the mouth and stomach. It is a sequential operation. For example, if *pepsin*, the enzyme secreted in the stomach during the first stage of protein digestion, has not converted these proteins into peptones, due to unfavorable conditions present in the stomach, then *erepsin*, the enzyme secreted in the intestine, will not be able to carry on the final stage of protein digestion, that of converting the peptones into amino acids. Each stage of digestion must not be interfered with, if we desire efficient digestion.

A third factor concerns the emptying time of the stomach into the intestine. Fruits remain in the stomach an hour or less, when eaten alone. Starches require two to three hours to complete gastric digestion. And proteins require approximately four hours. Some more complex foods, such as dried beans, are a rather difficult food to digest. Due to their high concentrations of both starch and protein, these foods may require five to six hours to complete gastric digestion. The important point here is this: If a food remains in the stomach longer than is normally required, due to an incompatible combination, the food will likely decompose, and nutrition is impaired.

So, considering all these factors of digestion, we may appreciate the importance of "food combining". And we may realize the potential of creating two very distinct situations when eating: one being digestion and nutrient enhancement; the other being decomposition of the food, a form of self-poisoning. If carbohydrates are not digested, they ferment, producing poisons such as carbon dioxide, acetic acid, lactic acid, and alcohol. (Note: The alcohol produced has the same potential for destruction of the liver and other organs, as commercial alcohol.) When proteins are not digested, they putrefy, producing poisons known as ptomaines and leucomaines.

Anytime two or more foods are eaten at the same meal, each one requiring opposite conditions for their digestion, the digestive process is less than efficient. Sometimes, digestion is totally suspended. The responsibility for harmonious digestion rests with each of us. Failure to observe the limitations of human digestion results in mild to severe indigestion and is very likely to be a contributing factor in causing disease.

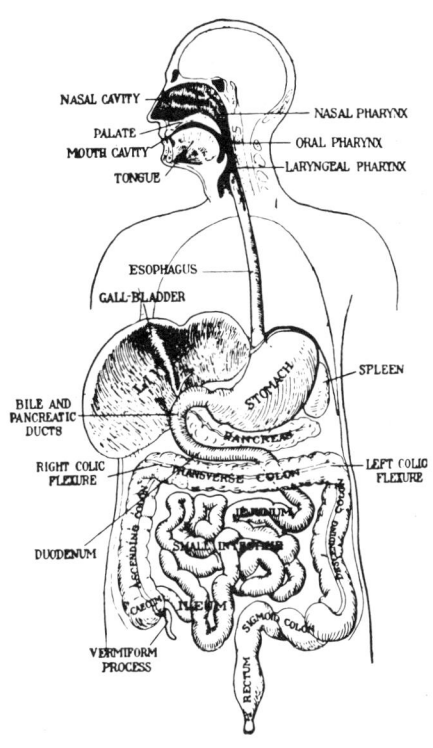

CLASSIFICATION OF FOODS

Proteins

nuts & seeds
peanuts
lentils
soybeans
dried beans
dried peas
garbanzo bean sprouts
lentil sprouts
sunflower sprouts
milk
cheese
eggs
flesh foods

Starches

potatoes
sweet potatoes
fresh lima beans
Globe artichokes
chestnuts
yams
winter squash
pumpkins
coconuts
cereals & grains
sprouted grains
mature, starchy corn
carrots
beets
parsnips
salsify

Fats

avocados
vegetable oils
butter
cream
margarine
lard

Acid Fruits

orange
grapefruit
pineapple
strawberry
kiwi
tomato
kumquat
lemon
lime
pomegranate

Sub-acid Fruits

mango
cherry
apple
peach
plum
apricot
berries
most grapes
pear
nectarine

Sweet Fruits

banana
date
persimmon
sapote
fresh fig
Thompson grapes
Muscat grapes
papaya
dried fruits

Low & Non-starchy vegetables

celery
fresh, sweet corn
fresh, sweet peas
Brussels sprouts
Chinese cabbage
broccoli
sweet pepper
summer squash
eggplant
alfalfa sprouts
green beans
garlic

lettuce
spinach
cucumber
cauliflower
cabbage
collards
bok choy
kohlrabi
turnips
kale
asparagus
onions

Melons

watermelon
honeydew
muskmelon
cantaloupe
casaba
crenshaw
Christmas melon
Persian melon
Canary melon

Note: Flesh foods and dairy products are not recommended as healthful food items. However, they are included for those who continue to eat them. Their digestibility will be enhanced by the application of "food combining" principles. Likewise, garlic and onions are best avoided, or used sparingly, as they irritate the digestive tract.

INCOMPATIBLE COMBINATIONS

Here are the combinations that are least compatible with the human digestive system. Although these combinations are commonly eaten, they are also quite often followed by the symptoms of indigestion. Familiarize yourself with them, and soon, selecting compatible food combinations will be easily attained.

Acid/Starch Combination

All acids destroy the starch-splitting enzyme, *salivary amylase*. This includes the acids contained in fruits and the acetic acid contained in vinegar. Additionally, the fruits will be detained in the stomach, resulting in fermentation.

Protein/Starch Combination

As stated earlier, *salivary amylase* is destroyed in the stomach in the presence of a highly acidic medium. Since protein digestion requires such a medium, this combination is unacceptable. (Note: since this combination is so commonly eaten, it may be a factor as to why "food combining" has not been recognized by conventional nutritionists as it contradicts many of our typical conventional meals.)

Protein/Protein Combination

Each type of protein food requires different timing and different modifications of the digestive secretions. When one protein is combined with another protein, digestion becomes difficult. As protein is the most difficult food nutrient for the body to digest anyway, we would benefit by consuming only one type of protein at a meal. This would not exclude the eating of two or more types of nuts at a meal, as their composition is relatively similar. (Note: The most recent data concerning protein needs has shown that it is unnecessary to consume all essential amino acids at each meal.)

Acid/Protein Combination

The renowned physiologist, Pavlov, demonstrated the influence of acids upon protein digestion. The enzyme, *pepsin*, necessary for protein digestion, will only be active in the presence of one particular acid, hydrochloric acid. Other acids may actually destroy this enzyme, including fruit acids. Also, when fruits are eaten with proteins, the fruits will, once again, be detained in the stomach until the completion of protein digestion, resulting in their fermentation.

There is an exception to this rule. The proteins such as nuts, seeds, and cheese, do not decompose as rapidly as other proteins, due to their high fat content. The inhibiting effect of fat on the gastric digestion of protein causes these types of proteins to receive their strongest digestive juice during the latter part of digestion. Therefore, the fruit acids do not delay the secretion of gastric juice any more than the fat content of these particular proteins. This distinction makes it acceptable to eat acid fruits with nuts, seeds, or cheese.

Fat/Protein Combination

As was mentioned in the preceding paragraph, fats inhibit the flow of gastric juice, interfering with protein digestion. Dr. Shelton referred to this in his book, by quoting from McLeod's *Physiology In Modern Medicine*: "Fat has been shown to exert a distinct inhibiting influence on the secretion of gastric juice...the presence of oil in the stomach delays the secretion of juice poured out on a subsequent meal of otherwise readily digestible food." Since our need for fat is very little, and most protein foods already contain a sufficient quantity of fat, any additional fat intake becomes difficult to digest. Avoid combining butter, oils, avocado, etc. with protein foods.

Sugar/Protein Combination

Sugars also inhibit the secretion of gastric juice, interfering with protein digestion. This is true of both fruit sugars and commercial sugars. And, the sugar will be detained in the stomach, once again, resulting in fermentation.

Sugar/Starch Combination

If starch is combined with sugar, the starch is disguised, preventing the adaptation of the saliva to starch digestion. That is, the saliva will not contain the enzyme, *salivary amylase*, necessary for starch digestion. And the sugars will ferment in the stomach. The common practice of pastry eating, or the common breakfast of mixing fruits with cereals or bread is a cause of various unpleasant symptoms.

Take Milk Alone

Milk is that perfect food provided by nature for the young of each mammalian species of animal. The nutrient content is specific to provide for the nutritional needs of the particular animal. For instance, the milk of the cow is suited to the specific needs of the growing calf. And human milk is suited to the specific needs of the human infant. However, there comes a time when the animal weans itself from its mother's milk. We would be wise to adopt such a plan, as the enzyme, *rennin*, secreted to digest milk proteins, is present in sufficient quantities only in the gastric juice of infants. When the child has a full set of teeth, the secretion of *rennin* begins to diminish. This phenomenon indicates the time for weaning and feeding solid food.

However, for those of you who want to continue using milk as a food item, please note that due to its protein and fat content, it combines poorly with all foods. Upon entering the stomach it forms curds which tend to form around the rest of the food in the stomach. This insulating effect prevents the digestion of the other foods until the milk curd is digested. Acid fruits constitute a fair combination with milk, but it is best to take it alone, and it is inadvisable to use it at all. (This rule also applies to soured milk, such as clabber or yogurt.)

FRUIT EATING

The human anatomy and physiology is most similar to those primates known as the anthropoid apes. These animals thrive on a diet consisting primarily of fruits and vegetation. They are classified as "frugivores", rather than "carnivores" (animals that kill and eat other animals) or "herbivores" (animals that feed on grasses). Humans are also naturally "frugivorous", as a study of our anatomy and physiology shows.* In other words, fruits and vegetables are our <u>natural primary foods</u>. In fact, by eating fruits to satisfy your needs for sugar, and vegetables to satisfy your needs for sodium, the desire for processed foods, containing refined sugar and non-usable salt, will greatly diminish. This chapter will instruct you on the compatible combinations of fruits.

Here is an excerpt from Dr. Shelton's book, commenting on fruit eating: "Fruits are among the finest and best of foods. Nothing affords us more good eating pleasure than a rich, mellow apple, a luscious, well-ripened banana, a carefully selected buttery, creamy, smooth avocado, or the wholesome, heart-warming goodness of a sweet grape. Real gustatory happiness is derived from the peach brought to the point of ripe perfection. Fruits, indeed, are a taste-enchanting, treasure trove of delightful eating enjoyment. With their luxury blends of rare flavors, delightful aromas, eye-pleasing colors, fruits are always an invitation to pleasure in eating."

Fruits may be relished in their natural state, i.e. whole, unseasoned, and uncooked. They supply us with an abundance of nutrients in the most easily assimilated form. Their carbohydrates are in the form of simple sugars; their proteins are in the form of amino acids; and their fats are in the form of fatty acids. These nutrients are ready for absorption, not requiring the energy expenditure of the digestive process. This fact concerning fruit digestion requires that they be eaten by themselves as an entire meal. This will allow them to be quickly sent to the small intestine where their nutrients may be readily absorbed.

However, if fruits are eaten with other foods, they will be detained in the stomach until the other food is digested, and the fruit sugars will ferment. This creates gastric disharmony, to say the least, and the fruits are unjustly blamed for the problem. The common practice of eating fruit with cereal, as in the conventional breakfast, or eating fruit as a "dessert", are examples of haphazard fruit eating.

Let's determine how fruits should be eaten. In terms of "food combining", fruits may be conveniently divided into three sub-classes: acid, sub-acid, and sweet. Determining which sub-class a particular fruit belongs is somewhat arbitrary. (See "Classification of Foods".) Combining fruits from the different sub-classes may or may not be compatible. Those of the sub-acid group may be combined with either the acid group or the sweet group. However, acid fruits should not be combined with sweet fruits, as the acids will interfere with the sweet fruits by delaying their exit from the stomach. Also, it's probably best to limit the types of fruits eaten at a meal to two or three. If the fruit has matured on the tree or vine and is fully ripened, one type of fruit may be totally satisfying.

Melons comprise an additional class of fruit, as they decompose even faster than other fruits. For this reason, it's been advised to eat melons separately from other fruits.

An unusual fruit, the avocado, provides us with an excellent natural source of fat. It combines best with non-starchy vegetables, and makes a fair combination with acid fruits. Its combination with sweet fruits is best avoided, due to the inhibiting effect of fat upon sugar. It also makes a fair combination with starches, due to its low protein content. It should definitely not be combined with proteins, as explained in the preceding chapter.

The tomato, although generally thought to be a vegetable, is really an acid fruit. Due to its low sugar content, it may be combined with non-starchy vegetables. As is the case with other acids, they should not be combined with either starches or proteins, except for those foods noted earlier: nuts, seeds, avocado, and cheese.

Fruits, except melons, may be combined with either lettuce or celery, as these vegetables are neutral in digestive chemistry. In fact, in cases of impaired digestion, they may enhance digestion of the fruits, especially the concentrated sweet varieties.

If fruit or vegetable juices are desired, they should be considered as an entire meal, or taken about 20 minutes before a meal. Since they dilute the digestive secretions, they should not be taken with a meal.

A final thought regarding the fruit meal is that it provides us with a natural "fast foods" selection. Simply prepared and served, they make the ideal breakfast for both children and adults. Rather than burdening your digestive system with a difficult task, your body may use its energy for other mental and/or physical activities of the day. So keep the above rules in mind and enjoy your frugivorous heritage.

*For further information regarding comparative anatomy and physiology and how it relates to the natural human diet, please read <u>Fit</u> <u>Food</u> <u>For</u> <u>Humanity</u>. Send $2.25 to Natural Hygiene Press, P.O. Box 30630, Tampa, FL 33630.

MEAL PLANNING

Let's get acquainted with this new way of eating. For some of you, this may be an easy change; for others, more difficult. The main objective is to keep the meals simple, yet enjoyable and satisfying.

Let's start with breakfast. Though generally taken immediately upon arising, it's unnecessary to do so. In fact, it's wise to wait on breakfast until hunger is present. This may be hours into the morning. Fruit makes the ideal food for breakfast, as it will not burden the digestive system with a heavy task. Just choose those fruits that are appealing to your senses, opting for those in season, as their quality and taste are highest at this time.

You may notice a difference between eating fruit as an entire meal, as opposed to just an occasional snack. For instance, you may realize it becomes necessary to consume a greater quantity of fruit than you have previously been accustomed to. Trust your appetite for the fruit and eat till you feel satisfied.

Lunch may consist of another fruit meal. Or vegetables may be desired. Again, trust your senses in making the choice. When choosing vegetables, remember that many of them are quite enjoyable eaten whole and uncooked such as tomatoes, cucumbers, bell peppers, fresh corn, celery, fresh sweet peas, lettuce (Romaine is my favorite), spinach, carrots, broccoli, cauliflower, and various sprouted grains or beans. Some vegetables may be preferred by lightly steaming them. Always have some fresh uncooked vegetables with the cooked food, as it will provide your body with an abundance of nutrients that are easily assimilated. Its probably best to limit the variety of vegetables to not more than four types at a meal.

If you desire something more concentrated with your vegetables, an avocado makes a good combination. Or you may desire a starch item such as potatoes, yams, or rice. One choice is best so as to avoid overeating on concentrated foods. Another possibility would be a protein choice. (Remember, do not include tomatoes in your meal if you intend to have either a starch or protein, with the exception of those proteins noted earlier.)

When preparing vegetables, it is best kept to a minimum. Many vegetables may just be washed and eaten whole. If a fruit or vegetable salad is preferred, avoid dicing and shredding, as these practices promote oxidation and a subsequent loss of nutritive value.

Salad greens may be cut in half and placed in a bowl, tossing them with other vegetables. The customary fashion of adding a "dressing" to the salad may be acceptable, but those commonly used are unhealthy. (All types of vinegar are highly toxic and should not be added to food. Also, once vegetable oil has been separated from its original source, the body has a difficult task in digesting it. Rather, it tends to coat the foods, preventing access by the digestive fluids.) As your taste buds become more sensitive, the enjoyment of simple foods increases. However, if you do desire a "dressing", see the one listed in the recipe section.

Dinner, the last meal of the day, may often be the best time to eat concentrated foods. Since the day's activities have been accomplished, there is more energy available to digest them. These concentrated foods should always be accompanied by whole, uncooked vegetables, especially the green leafy varieties.

It should be understood that although people commonly eat three meals a day, it may be more food than your body can efficiently digest. In fact, you may be better nourished on two meals rather than three. Two meals allows the body more time between meals to rest the digestive system, a significant factor in maintaining a well nourished body. Many factors must be weighed to determine whether two or three meals is more appropriate. A sedentary person will not need as much food as a more active one. In either case, it's best to eat when you feel hungry, rather than just because the clock indicates mealtime. If hunger is absent at any time, it's always best to skip the meal. (Although hunger is commonly associated with unpleasant feelings in the stomach, true hunger is actually felt as a pleasant sensation in the mouth and throat.)

Remember, allow sufficient time between meals to digest the previous meal. After fruit meals, allow 2-3 hours; after starch meals, allow 4 hours; and after protein meals, allow 6 hours. Your digestive system works best when it's given a rest between meals. The idea of eating "one meal all day long" is not a good one. Avoid the "snack" habit and your meals will prove to be more satisfying.

Dr. Vivian Vetrano, former director of Dr. Shelton's Health School, commented on this in an article she wrote for Dr. Shelton's "Hygienic Review". She stated, " It is not possible to have good digestion when eating too frequently. If the small intestine is not ready to receive food, reflex action will cause a slower emptying time of the stomach, holding the present meal in the stomach longer than ordinarily, thus favoring bacterial decomposition, instead of normal digestion. Furthermore, when the stomach is filled before the previous meal has been completely digested in the small intestine, peristalsis increases in the intestines, hurrying along the previous meal to make way for the present meal. Consequently, the previous meal will not remain in the upper small intestine long enough for perfect digestion or absorption. When we eat all day long, much of the food is just passed through the intestinal tract undigested and unabsorbed. One who indulges in food too frequently is overworking the glands and muscles of the body simply for the palliation of symptoms, or for the pleasure of the taste buds. This type of eating leads eventually and invariably to enervation, toxemia, disease, and premature death.

"We sometimes fail to appreciate the fact that digestion is muscular work, and eating all day long, by partaking frequently of snacks, keeps these muscles contracting so frequently that fatigue is inevitable, and future contractions are weaker, causing stasis of food in the digestive tube which may result in constipation. Eating after your regular evening meal, means that you are taking in more food than actually required, and burdening the body with more work when it ordinarily would begin its night of repose. If the evening meal is an extra meal, that means overwork, but if it is part of your daily eating schedule, then it was necessary and the nutritive value received compensates for the work of digestion.

"Unfortunately, there are so many opportunities to eat in modern life that no one gives himself a chance to get hungry. You may think that you are hungry when you are tired, if you have a headache, or if your stomach growls like a lion or gnaws like a rat, but these are abnormal conditions and not true hunger. Many are afraid of not getting a sufficient supply of nutrients in the day so they constantly stuff themselves. Some have decided they have hypoglycemia because of having read an article on this popular new myth, and they place themselves on six meals a day because this is what they have read is good. Consequently, poor digestion is the rule instead of the exception.

"It is a cardinal sin to put food in a stomach that is not ready for it. It is the same as stoking a furnace when there is already enough fuel. You crowd both systems, and in the furnace complete combustion does not take place and in the body, complete digestion is impossible."

Drinking with meals is another consideration. It's been shown that this practice dilutes the digestive juices, consequently retarding digestion. The best way to avoid this situation is to eliminate the use of salt and other condiments, and adopt a diet predominating in uncooked foods. This will result in a substantial reduction in your need for water. In fact, such a diet may provide you with all the water your body needs. Let thirst be your guide. However, if water is desired, it's best taken about 15 minutes before a meal. Or, if it's desired after a meal, it's best to wait one-half hour after a fruit meal; two hours after a starch meal; and four hours after a protein meal.

Keep in mind that the more variety of foods at a meal, the more likely to overeat, as each food item stimulates the appetite with its own unique taste sensation. You may feel quite satisfied and yet if another food is introduced, your appetite is once again aroused. In Dr. Shelton's words, "variety is the spice of gluttony." This advice is also applicable in regards to the destructive habit of having "dessert". As these generally contain sugar, they interfere with the digestion of the main meal. Better to satisfy your sugar desires during your fruit meals.

SEASONAL MENUS

Here are some suggestions for compatible food combinations, considering the availability of various foods at different times of the year.

Spring & Summer Menus

Breakfast	Lunch	Dinner
strawberries	cantaloupe	Romaine lettuce tomatoes avocado
cherries apricots	watermelon	Romaine lettuce broccoli almonds
peaches nectarines	honeydew melon	spinach & celery fresh, sweet corn brown rice
plums	fresh figs	green leaf lettuce cauliflower potatoes
crenshaw melon	bananas	red leaf lettuce cucumber pistachios
Canary melon	tomatoes Romaine lettuce avocado	celery spinach sweet potatoes

Autumn & Winter Menus

Breakfast	Lunch	Dinner
apples pears	Concord grapes	butter lettuce cauliflower yams
bananas dates celery stalks	persimmons	Romaine lettuce bell peppers pecans, filberts
kiwis oranges	tomatoes avocados Romaine lettuce	vegetable salad carrots brown rice
grapefruit tangelos	vegetable salad potatoes	vegetable salad cucumber lentils
bananas	tangerines pineapple avocado	Romaine lettuce broccoli mixed nuts
grapefruit	vegetable salad sweet potatoes	celery Brazil nuts tomatoes

CLOSING THOUGHTS

Remember, "food combining" represents only one factor of a healthful lifestyle. Incorporate it into your daily eating habits at your own pace, continually striving for improvement. Do not allow it to become a source of anxiety for yourself or those around you, especially at mealtime. Your meals should always be a thoroughly enjoyable experience. A serene atmosphere, both outside yourself and within, is of primary importance for good digestion. Remember, health is the objective, and simplicity is the key.

RECIPES

For those of you who desire to add a bit more of the culinary art to your meals and yet maintain the compatibilty of "food combining" principles, the following recipes have been created for your enjoyment. So, if you're in the creative food mood and wish to delight your palate while loving your tummy, take advantage of these tasteful and refreshing suggestions.

But first, here are a few remarks to clarify the use of particular items mentioned in the recipes:

* Water should either be distilled or soft spring water.
* The use of butter in some recipes is admittedly a compromise from the ideal. Please choose raw and unsalted.
* Vegetable oils should be "cold-pressed".
* Seasoning, if desired, should not contain salt or other inorganic minerals.

Remember to include an abundance of fresh, uncooked vegetables with these entrees, especially greens, with the exception of the fruit recipes.

CARROT PIE

1 large onion, chopped
10 carrots, sliced
2 tbsp. butter
Enough whole grain pie dough for top and bottom of shell.

Prepare dough. Steam carrots until soft, then mash them. And onions and butter. Place mixture into bottom of pie shell. Add crust top. Bake at 350 degrees until pie shell is light brown on top, about 25 minutes. Serve.

GREEN BEAN & ASPARAGUS SALAD

1 cup asparagus, steamed, cooled, cut into pieces
1/2 lb green beans prepared as asparagus above
3 celery stalks, chopped
1 cup mung sprouts
1/2 head green cabbage, cut up
3 large tomatoes, cut into pieces
1 handful dulse, torn. Rinse and drain in strainer.

Steam the asparagus and beans separately, as beans take longer. Let cool and cut up, not too small. Add all ingredients together in bowl with steamed vegies and top with avocado dressing (see page 62).

NOODLES STROGANOFF

4 cups cooked whole grain noodles
1 cup mushrooms, sliced
1 onion, chopped
1 cup sour cream
3 tbsp. butter or oil

Heat skillet with 1 tbsp. butter. When heated, add mushrooms and onion. Stir with a little water until cooked. Add 1 cup sour cream and butter. Spread over noodles and serve.

TROPICAL SUMMER FRUIT SALAD

4 peaches or nectarines
8 apricots, pitted
3 ripe bananas
1 mango
1 papaya

Cut fruit over bowl to secure juice and serve.

NUTTY VEGIE SALAD

1 bunch chives chopped very small
1 head romaine lettuce, torn
1 bunch spinach, torn
2 small summer squash, cut
3 stalks celery, chopped
2 or 3 tomatoes, or 1 cup cherry tomatoes
1 cup snow peas, stems remove, steamed and cooled
1 cup asparagus, steamed and cooled
1 cup broccoli tops, steamed and cooled
1 cup sunflower seeds -- sunflower seed oil, enough to moisten salad

Mix items together in bowl. Moisten with sunflower oil and serve.

LENTIL SOUP

2 cups dry lentils
4 cups water
1 bunch green onions, chopped
1 cup grated carrot
3 carrots sliced into large sections
5 stalks celery, including tops

Bring water to boil, add lentils, turn heat to simmer, cook 25 minutes. Add vegetables, cook another 15 minutes. When done, add seasoning if desired.

FROZEN PERSIMMON PUDDING

5 ripened "soft-style" persimmons, frozen
5 very ripe bananas, frozen
2 cups sweet, seedless grapes, frozen

Thaw slightly. Smash persimmons and bananas together. Sprinkle whole grapes on top. Serve.

YUMMY YAMMY PIE

Prepare enough whole grain pie dough for top and bottom.

1 cup chestnuts, steamed, peeled, and chopped into small pieces.
5 medium yams, cooked well. Remove tips.
1/2 cup cream
1/2 stick butter

Prepare bottom of pie crust into pan. Smash entire yams including skins. Add cream and butter to yams to make a soft, whipped texture. Add chestnut pieces. Fill pie shell with filling of yams, cream, and butter. Put on crust top and bake at 350 degrees for 30 minutes.

STARCHED JACKETS

5 baked potatoes
5 baked yams, remove tips
2 large avocados
4 celery stalks, cut fine

Slice off a top "cap" of each potato and take out insides. Place filling in bowl. Add yams with their skins to bowl. Mix all the fillings together with mashed avocado. Add celery and stir all together. Place mixture back into potato jackets. Serve.

CITRUS DELUXE SALAD

5 navel oranges, cut into pieces
2 grapefruit, cut into pieces
1 pineapple, cut into cubes
1 cup strawberries, sliced

Place fruit into bowl. Juice 2 oranges and pour juice over salad to moisten.

VEGIE TACOS

1 medium onion, chopped
2 cups cooked millet
1 tsp. cummin powder (optional)
1 cup corn
1 broccoli head, chopped
1 bell pepper chopped fine
2 tbsp. butter
2 tbsp. vegetable oil

Prepare millet by cooking 2 cups millet and 2 cups water until water is absorbed and millet soft. Steam broccoli until half done and place in pan with 2 tbsp. oil and other vegies to saute over medium heat. Stir until done. Add butter for flavor after sauteing. Heat tortillas in oven until warmed. Fill tortillas with vegie/millet mix. Add seasoning if desired.

SEABREEZE SALAD

1 handful snow peas
1 head romaine lettuce
1/2 head iceberg lettuce
1 handful dulse, torn. Rinse and drain in strainer.
1/2 bunch spinach
1 cup cherry tomatoes or chopped tomato
5 small cucumbers, sliced chunky
8 oz. fresh pecan meats, whole or chopped
4 oz. alfalfa sprouts
lemon juice to moisten (optional)

Mix vegies together in bowl. Add nuts and optional dressing.

MACARONI SALAD

1-1/2 cups noodles (whole wheat macaroni) cooked and cooled
1/4 cup green onion tops or chives, chopped fine
1 bell pepper, chopped fine
1 head romaine lettuce
1/2 head iceberg lettuce
1/2 bunch spinach, chopped well
1 cup grated carrot
1 cup peas, (if frozen, thaw; if fresh use raw or steam lightly)
1 cup corn, prepared same as peas

Prepare noodles and cool. Prepare peas and corn. Mix all ingredients together in a bowl and add avocado dressing (see recipe page 62).

TOFU AND VEGETABLES

1 lb. tofu, rinsed and towel dried
1 bell pepper, chopped
15 snow peas, whole
1 bunch green onions, chopped
2 stalks celery, chopped large
2 zuccini, sliced
5 mushrooms, sliced
1/2 cup broccoli tops, cut small
1/2 bunch spinach
2 tbsp. oil

Place oil in pan on medium heat. When oil is hot, add tofu and all vegies together, except spinach. Add 1-2 cups water and stir frequently. Add lid and turn to simmer. When almost done, place spinach leaves on top and simmer until spinach is done.

VEGIE PIE WITH CRUST

Prepare enough whole grain pie dough for a top and bottom.

4 medium potatoes, chunked
3 large carrots, sliced
1 bunch green onion tops, chopped fine
1 cup peas
2 stalks celery, including tops
1 large onion, chopped
2 tbsp. butter

Place bottom of pie crust in pan. Steam potatoes until half done. Add celery, carrots, peas, and onions to potatoes. Place all in pie shell. Slice 2 tbsp. butter over top of vegies. Place top of crust on pie. Bake at 350 degrees for 30 minutes. Serve.

GUACAMOLE

4 ripe avocados
2-3 tsp. chives, chopped (optional)
2 tomatoes
1 large cucumber
1/2 cup alfalfa sprouts
lemon juice to taste
1 bunch romaine lettuce

Mash avocados and add other vegie pieces to this. Mix in alfalfa sprouts and lemon juice to vegies. Add seasoning if desired. Spread over lettuce leaves, folding over to make lettuce sandwiches. Use celery sticks to dip into guacamole.

RICE STUFFED CABBAGE

2 very large-leafed cabbages
3 cups cooked rice
1 onion, chopped
7 mushrooms, sliced
3 tbsp. butter

Steam cabbage until leaves fall from bunch or can be pulled off easily. Cook mushrooms and onion in skillet with 1 tbsp. butter and a little water. When done mix with cooked rice, seasoning, and butter. Place a few spoonfuls of the rice-mushroom mixture in each cabbage leaf, folding and overlapping 4 sides of the leaves to the center. Place "bundles" in steamer upside down and steam for 30 minutes on low heat. Serve.

RICE SALAD

1/2 cup chestnuts, baked or steamed, then peeled and chopped
2 avocados
1 cup cooked brown rice, cooled
1 head romaine lettuce, torn
1/2 bunch spinach, torn
1 cup grated carrot
1 red bell pepper, chopped fine green onion (tops only), chopped fine
1/8 cup parsley, chopped fine
1/2cup peas
1 cup alfalfa sprouts

Prepare chestnuts and cool. Prepare rice and cool. Mix vegies and rice together in a large bowl. Add avocado dressing (see page 62) and mix together. Sprinkle chestnut pieces over top and serve.

LENTIL ARTICHOKE SURPRISE

2 cups lentil sprouts
1 broccoli head, cut in pieces
4 artichokes
2 stalks celery, cut fine
1 head romaine lettuce

Steam artichokes. Remove leaves and cut hearts into pieces. Steam lentil sprouts and broccoli. Mix all the above together. Add finely chopped celery. Serve on lettuce leaves or wrap lettuce around mixture to make "sandwich".

SEAWEED SOUP

1 loose cup arame seaweed
2 onions
4 carrots
1 yam
3 potatoes

Rinse seaweed well, soak 1/2 hour drain well. Slice onions into rings. Chop carrots, yam, and potatoes into pieces. Steam carrots, yam, potatoes, and onions until almost done. Place in soup pot, add 2 cups water, add seaweed, cook 10-15 minutes until simmering. Serve.

TOSTADAS

2 ripe avocados
1 bunch spinach
1/4 cup chives, chopped
1 bunch broccoli tops, chopped chunky
1/2 cup peas
6-8 corn tortillas
2 cups alfalfa sprouts

Lightly steam vegies. Place corn tortillas in oven at 450 degrees until crispy. Add mashed avocado on each tortilla. Add steamed vegies on top, then add grated carrot and sprouts on top. Season if desired. Serve.

FRUIT BALLS

1 cup raisins
1 cup pitted dates
1/4 cup carob powder (optional)
2 ripe bananas
2 apples or pears, diced

Smash bananas and add other ingredients and roll into balls, adding slight amount of water if necessary. Place balls on wax paper on cookie sheet and refrigerate until hard. Serve.

CAULIFLOWER AND MILLET BOWL

1 cauliflower, steamed
1 cup cooked millet
1 avocado

Smash cauliflower and avocado together with fork and add to millet and mix together well in bowl. Serve.

SWEET AUTUMN SALAD

4 apples
4 pears
5 ripe bananas
1/2 cup raisins
1/2 cup date pieces
1/3 cup apple juice

Slice and mix fruits together. Moisten the mixture with apple juice poured over it. Serve.

BAKED FRENCH FRIES

Preheat oven to 450 degrees. Slice potatoes 1/4" thin and place in large bowl. Pour cold press oil on palms of hands and rub all over potatoes to moisten. Place on cookie sheet, bake until lightly crispy on one side, then turn over to do other side.

POTATO SALAD

1 cup corn
4 lbs potatoes
3 avocados
2 cups peas
1 bell pepper, chopped
7 celery stalks, chopped
1 carrot, grated

Cook potatoes 2 hours before meal, by steaming until done but not too soft. Allow to cool in refrigerator. Cut potatoes in cubes and add to all the vegies in a bowl. Add avocado dressing (see recipe page 62) and stir up mixture together. Serve.

BROWN RICE STUFFED BELL PEPPERS

3 cups rice
3 cups water
4 green or red peppers
1 onion, chopped
7 mushrooms
2 zuccini or other summer squash
2 medium avocados (optional)

Cook rice and keep warm. Steam peppers until fairly soft. Cut a hole at top of each pepper and remove stem and seeds. Cook other vegies in skillet with 1 tbsp. vegetable oil and a little water at medium heat. Mix rice and vegies together with mashed avocado and fill peppers with this mixture.

FROZEN BANANA CREME

This recipe requires a Champion juicer

Buy and peel fully ripened bananas.
Freeze hard in plastic bag or container.

Install the solid plastic panel beneath the juicer barrel, and place a bowl beneath the juicer spout.

Feed frozen bananas into juicer. Serve and enjoy the amazing taste and consistency of this treat and its similarity to ice cream.

AVOCADO SALAD DRESSING

Mash avocados into a smooth consistency, thinning with a small amount of water. (Lemon juice may be used instead of water if starch is not being served with the meal.) Use as a spread over the vegetable salad. (Do not use this with a protein meal, as avocados combine very poorly with proteins.)

LETTERS FROM THANKFUL READERS

"Thank you for <u>Food</u> <u>Combining</u> <u>Simplified</u>. In a few days of following the correct principles, I have been relieved of painful gas and indigestion problems."
-- Renee Ramos, Hilo, HI.

"I have read <u>Food</u> <u>Combining</u> <u>Simplified</u>. It is exactly what I needed. My physical and mental improvement is overwhelming."-- Carol Thomas, Garfield, AR.

"I really wanted to thank you and congratulate you for a job well done in the book <u>Food</u> <u>Combining</u> <u>Simplified</u>. Having studied nutrition and pre-medical courses in college, I came away from it all believing that the whole subject of nutrition was too obscure and unapproachable because of the many opinions on the matter. And then your book--concise, small, easy to read (and reread), and certainly housing the most sensible information on the subject that I've seen. I picked up your book about four months ago and have followed your suggestions pretty much to a tee....I've managed to lose over 50 pounds during that time but more importantly I feel much better and I have more energy too. Again, I thank you, thank you, thank you." -- Mitchell Donahue, Montgomeryville, PA.

If you cannot obtain a copy of Food Combining Simplified locally, send $3.00 to D. Nelson, P.O. Box 2302, Santa Cruz, CA 95063.

Food Combining Simplified is available to anyone at a wholesale discount. Send $15.00 to D. Nelson, P.O. Box 2302, Santa Cruz, CA 95063 and receive 10 copies postpaid.

Food Combining Made Easy by Dr. Herbert Shelton is available from Natural Hygiene Press, P.O. Box 30630, Tampa, FL 33630. $4.50 postpaid.